COLLECTION EDITOR & DESIGN *CORY LEVINE*
ASSISTANT EDITORS *ALEX STARBUCK* & *NELSON RIBEIRO*
EDITORS, SPECIAL PROJECTS *JENNIFER GRÜNWALD* & *MARK D. BEAZLEY*
SENIOR EDITOR, SPECIAL PROJECTS *JEFF YOUNGQUIST*
SVP OF DIGITAL & PRINT PUBLISHING SALES *DAVID GABRIEL*

EDITOR IN CHIEF *AXEL ALONSO*
CHIEF CREATIVE OFFICER *JOE QUESADA*
PUBLISHER *DAN BUCKLEY*
EXECUTIVE PRODUCER *ALAN FINE*

DAREDEVIL BY MARK WAID VOL. 4. Contains material originally published in magazine form as DAREDEVIL #16-21. First printing 2013. Hardcover ISBN# 978-0-7851-6102-8. Softcover ISBN# 978-0-7851-6103-5. Published by MARVEL WORLDWIDE, INC., a subsidiary of MARVEL ENTERTAINMENT, LLC. OFFICE OF PUBLICATION: 135 West 50th Street, New York, NY 10020. Copyright © 2012 and 2013 Marvel Characters, Inc. All rights reserved. All characters featured in this issue and the distinctive names and likenesses thereof, and all related indicia are trademarks of Marvel Characters, Inc. No similarity between any of the names, characters, persons, and/or institutions in this magazine with those of any living or dead person or institution is intended, and any such similarity which may exist is purely coincidental. **Printed in the U.S.A.** ALAN FINE, EVP - Office of the President, Marvel Worldwide, Inc. and EVP & CMO Marvel Characters B.V.; DAN BUCKLEY, Publisher & President - Print, Animation & Digital Divisions; JOE QUESADA, Chief Creative Officer; TOM BREVOORT, SVP of Publishing; DAVID BOGART, SVP of Operations & Procurement, Publishing; RUWAN JAYATILLEKE, SVP & Associate Publisher, Publishing; C.B. CEBULSKI, SVP of Creator & Content Development; DAVID GABRIEL, SVP of Print & Digital Publishing Sales; JIM O'KEEFE, VP of Operations & Logistics; DAN CARR, Executive Director of Publishing Technology; SUSAN CRESPI, Editorial Operations Manager; ALEX MORALES, Publishing Operations Manager; STAN LEE, Chairman Emeritus. For information regarding advertising in Marvel Comics or on Marvel.com, please contact Niza Disla, Director of Marvel Partnerships, at ndisla@marvel.com. For Marvel subscription inquiries, please call 800-217-9158. **Manufactured between 12/31/2012 and 2/11/2013 (hardcover), and 12/31/2012 and 8/12/2013 (softcover), by R.R. DONNELLEY, INC., SALEM, VA, USA.**

10 9 8 7 6 5 4 3 2 1

WRITER
MARK WAID

ARTISTS
CHRIS SAMNEE
(#16 & #18-21)
MICHAEL ALLRED
(#17)

COLOR ARTISTS
JAVIER RODRIGUEZ
(#16 & #18-21)
LAURA ALLRED
(#17)

LETTERER
VC'S JOE CARAMAGNA

COVER ARTISTS
CHRIS SAMNEE (#16)
MICHAEL ALLRED (#17)
PAOLO RIVERA (#18-21)

ASSISTANT EDITOR
ELLIE PYLE

EDITOR
STEPHEN WACKER

BATTLIN' JACK MURDOCK WANTED HIS SON TO LIVE HIS LIFE WITHOUT FEAR.

HE URGED MATT NOT TO FOLLOW IN HIS FOOTSTEPS AS A SMALL-TIME BOXER...TO HAVE THE GUTS TO MAKE SOMETHING OF HIMSELF.

WHEN MATT WA STILL A TEENAG HE SAVED AN O MAN ABOUT TO RUN OVER BY RUNAWAY TRUC

BUT A RADIOACTIVE CYLINDER FELL FROM THE TRUCK AND BLINDED MATT FOR LIFE.

YET HE SOON REALIZED HIS OTHER SENSES HAD BECOME SUPERHUMANLY ACUTE!

HE COULD TELL WHETHER OR NOT SOMEONE WAS LYING BY LISTENING TO THE PERSON'S HEARTBEAT.

HE COULD RECOGNIZE PEOPLE BY SCENT ALONE.

AND HE HAD DEVELOPED A SIXTH SENSE, A RADAR-LIKE AWARENESS OF WHERE OBJECTS WERE.

MURDOCK DIDN'T NEED ANY SUPER-POWERS TO GRADUATE AT THE TOP OF HIS LAW SCHOOL CLASS.

HE BECAME A SUCCESSFUL ATTORNEY, FULFILLING THE DREAMS OF HIS FATHER.

BATTLIN' JACK DID NO LIVE LONG ENOUGH TO SAVOR MATT' SUCCESS.

GANGSTERS' BULLETS CUT HIM DOWN AFTER REFUSING TO THROW A FIGHT.

JACK DIDN'T WANT MATT TO BECOME A FIGHTER. BUT TO BRING HIS FATHER'S KILLERS TO JUSTICE, HE BECAME A MAN WITHOUT FEAR.

HERE COMES...

DAREDEVIL

This page by:
Fred Van Lente, Marcos Martin,
and Blambot's Nate Piekos

DAILY BUGLE

NEW YORK'S FINEST DAILY NEWSPAPER

SINCE 189...
★★★
$1.00 (in N...
$1.50 (outside...

INSIDE: CAPTAIN MARVEL CAPTIVATES MASS., VAMPIRE VEXATIONS, PUNISHER(S?!) PRESENCE PERS...

KNIGHT IN SHINING ARMOR

BLAM BLAM BLAM

Latveria issues statement regarding Iron Man's incursion into the country, denies allegations of Daredevil detainment.

MATT MURDOCK MISSING?

Manhattan's favorite blind lawyer, Matt Murdock, has been suspiciously absent from the legal (and singles!) scene. Could this have anything to do with the rumors that he's Daredevil?

(pictured here with law partner Foggy Nelson]

Remembering JANET VAN DYN...

Heiress, Avenger and wife to Giant-Ma... (Hank Pym)

YOU'RE *CLEAR* FOR ⸮KZZT⸮ MOMENT, HANK. TAKE A BREATH.

YEAH, NO. CAN'T *AFFORD* TO.

DIDN'T MATT ONCE SAY THAT HE GOT HIS HYPERSENSES FROM A DOSE OF RADIOACTIVE WASTE?

"THAT HE GOT HIT WHEN HE PUSHED AN OLD MAN OUT OF THE WAY OF A CAREENING TRUCK?"

WHAT OLD MAN?

WHAT *TRUCK?*

...

I HAVE ABSOLUTELY NO IDEA. WEIRD. SOMETHING... *FLASHED* THROUGH OUR *CONNECTION* LIKE A...

...LIKE A *NOISE* FROM ANOTHER *ROOM*...

HANG ON.

STILL THERE?

TALK TO ME!

MENTAL ECHOES. SEE, THAT'S WHAT'S ALARMING. I THINK...

...TONY, I THINK MATT'S BROAD-CASTING...!

MY BIOWARE'S SHOWING INCREDIBLE ENERGIES DOWN HERE RELATED TO HIS HYPERSENSES! I CAN FEEL MY SKIN TINGLING...EARS RINGING...LIKE HE MUST!

WHAT?

BLEEDING SIGNALS! TONY, SOMEHOW--TO THIS DAY--MATT'S SENSORY NODES, HIS BRAIN...THEY'RE STILL AMPED WITH TRACE RADIATION!

THEY'RE IN PEAK OVERLOAD STRAINING TO REACH PAST THE BLOCKAGE... AND IN MATT'S "ABSENCE"...

...THEY'RE CRACKLING IN THROUGH MY HELMET!

THAT'S NOT--

NO, IT ISN'T. I DON'T LIKE THIS! HANK, GET OUT OF THERE! NOW!

LOVE TO! UNFORTUNATELY, I'M SURROUNDED! THESE ARE AGGRESSIVE BUGS, MY FRIE--

HNNGGH!

HANK! HANK, ARE YOU THERE?

TONY, DO SOMETHING!

I WAS ALREADY IMPROVISING, OKAY? UNLESS YOU HAVE A MICROSCOPIC CELL PHONE ON YOU, LET ME THINK...!

...NNNNHH....
TUH... ...TONY...?
CAN YOU
HEAR ME?

TONY...?

TONY,
I'M IN *BAD*
TROUBLE
HERE.

WHERE...
WHERE'S THE
CANNON? IT
MUST BE
CLOSE--

HyaAAGGH!

ALONE. I'M ALONE.

HE'S HAVING A SEIZURE--!

THEN SPELL HIM AGAIN OR WHATEVER! HANK, IF YOU CAN HEAR ME, HANG ON--!

THIS... ...THIS IS WHAT IT'S LIKE FOR YOU, ISN'T IT, MATT?

A WORLD OF TERROR.

IN THE BLACKNESS...

...SHAPES MOVING...

I remember.

There's been an accident. A truck. An old man. I'm in the hospital.

They tell me I'm *blind* now.

But that's not *true*. Not *completely*.

Sometimes there are *blurry contours* in the air.

Monsters. Ghosts flickering at the edge of the darkness.

And I have never felt so terrified.

In time, the ghosts slowly morph and sharpen into things I can kind of recognize.

The silhouette of a *drip bag*.

The vague outline of my *father*.

And the fear gradually *subsides*.

Eventually, I come to find that I have a *gift*...a *form* of sight...a "*radar sense*" that, if I want to *live*...

...I HAVE TO *TRUST*...!

IT'S NO *USE!* THE MALFUNCTION'S ON *HIS* END! HE'S NOT *RECEIVING!*

TRY AN *ASTRAL PROJECTION* OR SOMETHING WHILE I PUT IN A CALL TO--

¿ZZT¿LO?

HANK! YOU *OKAY?*

I'M *ALIVE.* LOST MY *LIGHT,* BUT I'VE RIGGED THE CANNON TO LET OFF ENOUGH TO *NAVIGATE* WITH.

NANOBOTS ARE *CLEARED.* STRANGE, TALK ME *OUT* OF HERE.

"I'M *SPENT.*"

...NO SIGN OF SHOCK OR CONCUSSION, THAT'S GOOD...

...BREATHING'S NORMAL...

I'M FINE. I'M JUST...

...

WE *REALLY* UNDERESTIMATE THAT GUY.

THE PAIN AND THE FEAR HE HAD TO OVERCOME JUST TO FUNCTION...I HAD NO IDEA. YOU CAN'T *IMAGINE.*

I SUSPECT YOU CAN, HOWEVER. YOUR LIFE EXPERIENCES ARE...NOT DISSIMILAR.

THERE'S SOMETHING ELSE. I WONDER IF--

HNNNNNHH--!

PATIENT'S *AWAKE!*

WHERE... AM I...?

WHY DON'T YOU TELL *ME?*

Three familiar heartbeats. Dr. Strange, Hank Pym, and the metronomic rhythm of Tony Stark.

Smell of iron and perspiration. Feel of electronic vibration. Taste of filtered air. I'm in Stark's *lab.*

I'm back in the *world.*

Thank *God.*

Stark explains what happened to me--how the Latverians put me in sensory deprivation and how he and the others fixed it.

As usual when Tony talks, he can't stop himself from gesturing proudly towards an array of devices and inventions like I can see them.

I am polite about it.

In turn, I explain to Strange that deep inside my coma, I temporarily evolved some new senses to compensate.

His curiosity wanes when I tell him in no uncertain terms that they were not worth the hell I had to endure to stumble *into* them.

Already, their memory is eroding like a nightmare after waking. Everything else, I just chalk up to hallucination.

Most everything.

SO HOW LONG AGO WAS I KIDNAPPED? TWO DAYS? THREE?

NINE.

NINE?

I GOTTA GET *MOVING*, THEN. THANKS FOR *EVERYTHING*, GENTS.

¿TCH¿ SOMEDAY. RIGHT, ALYSSA?

I KNOW YOU'RE THERE, ALYSSA. I CAN SMELL YOUR PERFUME. ANY *CALLS*?

HELLO? *SOMEBODY* WANT TO SAY "HI"?

No one does.

And the air grows thick and lousy with the stench of adrenal cortisone and endorphins:

The smell of stress.

MATT, CAN I SEE YOU IN YOUR OFFICE, PLEASE?

And Foggy's voice has the tone of an undertaker's.

Now *I'm* stressed.

HEY, PARTNER. SORRY I HAVEN'T CALLED, BUT--

ARE YOU ALL RIGHT? ARE YOU INJURED IN ANY WAY THAT I SHOULD BE CONCERNED ABOUT?

CUT MY CHIN *SHAVING.* HURTS LIKE THE *DEV--*

NO? THEN *SIT THE HELL DOWN.* NOT BEHIND THE DESK. *THERE.*

I WAS *WAY* OUT OF TOWN. SORRY. EVERYTHING'S JAKE NOW. HOW'S THE *SISSAL* CASE COMING ALON--

I TOOK YOU OFF THE SISSAL CASE. I TOOK YOU OFF *EVERYTHING.* I PUT YOUR *APPOINTMENT BOOK* IN THE *SHREDDER.*

BECAUSE I HAD TO TAKE OFF ON *DAREDEVIL* BUSINESS? *COME ON!* WE'VE ALWAYS HAD *CONTINGENCIES* FOR THOSE SCENARIOS! THAT'S NOT *NEW!*

FOGGY, EITHER JOHN BONHAM IS DRUMMING ON YOUR CHEST, OR THAT'S YOUR *HEART* RACING. *WHAT IS UP?*

I CALLED IT.

CALLED *WHAT?*

YOUR MENTAL STATE.

YOU SAID YOU WERE *FINE* AFTER ALL THE *INSANITY* YOU'VE BEEN THROUGH THESE LAST FEW YEARS.

YOU ARGUED THAT "FAKE IT 'TIL YOU MAKE IT" WAS A VALID DEFENSE AGAINST ALL THE *CRAZINESS* AND *DEPRESSION.*

YOU *SWORE* TO ME THAT "*HAPPY MATT*" WAS YOU COPING *SUCCESSFULLY* WITH *DESPAIR.* BUT I KNOW YOU BETTER THAN ANYONE, AND I HATE IT WHEN YOU *LIE* TO YOURSELF...

...AND I HATE IT EVEN MORE WHEN YOU *LIE TO ME!*

THIS...

It is.

...THIS CAN'T...

I buried him with his gloves. The texture...every crack in the leather a *fingerprint*...

...CAN'T BE...

STOP LYING!

I HAVE TEST RESULTS! WHAT I *NEED* IS HONESTY SO WE CAN GET YOU SOME *HELP!*

FOGGY, YOU HAVE TO BELIEVE ME. I *DIDN'T*...THIS ISN'T WHAT IT...

....I HAVE ENEMIES. IT'S SOME SORT OF CRUEL *SETUP*, OR...

IT'S EVIDENCE, IS WHAT IT IS. IT'S EVERYTHING MY INSTINCTS HAVE BEEN *SCREAMING* AT ME. YOU'RE NOT...*RIGHT.* ONE LAST TIME, MATT...EITHER LET ME *HELP* YOU--

YOU CAN'T BE *SERIOUS!* I'M NOT THE *PROBLEM!*

--OR GET *OUT!*

EXCUSE ME?

I CAN'T DO THIS ANYMORE. I CAN'T TAKE CARE OF YOU *AND* MYSELF *AND* A LAW FIRM--

--YOU NEED TO *LEAVE.*

UNTIL SUCH TIME AS YOU'RE WILLING TO BE *STRAIGHT* WITH ME, I'VE DELEGATED YOUR WORKLOAD, I'M TAKING YOUR NAME OFF THE DOOR, AND I'M DEMANDING A BREAK.

THIS IS THE *CRAZY* PART. YOU'RE MY BEST FRIEND--!

I'M YOUR PUNCHING BAG. AND I AM JUST SO VERY TIRED OF IT. AND YOU HAVE FINALLY EXHAUSTED MY PATIENCE.

"YOU STILL WANT TO BE FRIENDS? THEN GET SOME *REAL HELP* AND STOP *PRETENDING* YOU'RE OKAY.

"UNTIL THEN...

NELSON & MURDOCK

ATTORNEYS AT LAW

NELSON & MURD

"...WE'RE *THROUGH.*"

IF YOU COULD HAVE YOUR SIGHT BACK, MATT...FOR JUST, LIKE, HALF AN HOUR...

...AND YOU COULD SEE *ONE THING* YOU *MISSED*, PAST OR PRESENT...

...WHAT WOULD IT BE?

THE GREAT DIVIDE

This street corner is a lot like my life:

Constantly being rebuilt from scratch because it keeps getting flattened.

About an hour ago, my best friend, Foggy Nelson, dissolved our law partnership and told me to lose his number.

He found my father's remains hidden in my *office* when they should be in his *coffin*, and I couldn't explain. *Can't* explain.

Now Foggy's convinced I'm either a liar or mentally unbalanced, *all evidence to the contrary.*

Like he doesn't know me at *all.*

I hope he's happy with the decision he's made, that sanctimonious--

--

Dial it down. He's not the bad guy here. And it's not the first time we've gone off the rails by not *trusting* one another.

I was reminded of that when, desperate to walk off my stress and confusion, I wandered here.

I think the last structure on this site was a noxious coffee shop that got deservedly vaporized during the Skrull invasion.

Time was, though...back when Nelson and Murdock set up in New York...

...our first office was here...

...and things weren't any smoother than they are today.

NELSON & MURDOCK
ATTORNEYS AT LAW

IT'S NOT CALLED A "PRACTICE" BECAUSE WE'RE ALLOWED DO-OVERS, FOGGY! WE'RE GETTING HAMMERED!

NOVICK WAS THE FOURTH CASE IN A ROW WE'VE LOST!

I'M SORRY... YOU'VE LOST, WHILE I WAS HANDLING MOST OF THE CASELOAD!

We were a little over a year in and at each other's throats.

Our office manager, who we both adored, had run off to Hollywood, and only in her absence did we realize how integral she'd been to peace and harmony.

I PROMISED MY DAD I'D GROW UP TO BE A LAWYER, NOT A LACKEY! WHAT IS THIS, A HOBBY TO YOU NOW?

WHOA! WHOA! WHOSE MONEY DID WE START THIS FIRM WITH? MINE!

THEN TAKE IT SERIOUSL WHEN KAREN LEFT, YOU D TOO! YOU'RE NEVER AROUND...I DON'T HAVE T TAKE OFF MY SHOES TO COUNT YOUR BILLABLE HOURS...

WHAT DO YOU DO WITH YOUR DAYS, "PARTNER"? YO HAVE SOME SORT OF DOUBLE LIFE I SHOULD KNOW ABOUT?

(Back then, Foggy wasn't aware I was Daredevil, so that irony was lost on him.

Which doesn't make it any less cheap a shot, but mitigates his retort:)

YOU KNOW, YOU'RE NOT EXACTLY MR. RELIABLE! YOU COME AND YOU GO...CLIENTS COMPLAIN...

I WISH YOU COULD SEE THE NONSENSE I DEAL WITH!

SO DO I.

--that a man in *hydraulic armor* had been sent to *kill* him?

THINK I'LL MAKE SURE NO ONE CAN *TELL* THEM!

AAAAAA!

DAREDEVIL?

HNNF!

LUCKY FOR *YOU*. IF I WAS *THOR*, YOU'D BE CHOKING FROM B.O.

FIND A *HIDING PLACE* AND *STAY* THERE! I'LL DEAL WITH HIM!

BILL 'N' WALT'S SHAKE SHOPPE

HE HAS MY *FILES*--

I SAID RUN FO YOUR LI MAN!

KRAKOOOM!

Which is not to say that he was a total *pushover.*

Despite his ludicrous appearance and one-note *schtick,* that hydraulic suit was *well-built.*

Like *Iron Man's* armor if it had been designed by *Napoleon.*

Sophisticated gyro-motors kept him upright--

--and he could move at *terrific* speed when he took *full strides.*

Also: strong.

My biggest mistake was allowing him to take the fight to the *water*.

Hydraulic fluid leaks *fast* when *pressurized.* Problem solved, question *unanswered.*

Again, why would anyone employ this buffoon as a burglar? He was the least subtle villain *ever.*

He couldn't travel with *any* level of *subterfuge.*

Bystanders staring, pointing... impossible to make a clean *escape...*

‡Koff‡ ...WHY *HIM?* WHY...

OH, MY *GOD.*

Why does *anyone* hire a man on stilts?

TO ATTRACT *ATTENTION.*

To create a *distraction*.

ALL AVAILABLE UNITS--ALL AVAILABLE UNITS--

PERP'S BEEN SPOTTED OVER BY *PIER 62!* HEADQUARTERS, SEND A *CONTAINMENT UNIT!*

ONE SIDE, PEOPLE! ONE SIDE!

HEY, *BUDDY!* WHAT WAS *THAT?* YOU *OKAY...?*

...THEN HE HANDED THESE TO *ME* AND SAID STILT-MAN HAD *STOLEN* THEM. IS *THAT* WHAT HAPPENED?

YEAH. GOD, DAREDEVIL'S A LIFE-SAVER.

LET'S SEE HOW HE IS AT SAVING *PARTNERSHIPS.*

THE WAITER READ ME A COUPLE OF NAMES OFF THESE FOLDERS. *PASKO* WAS ONE. *FORTKNIGHT,* THE OTHER.

NEITHER OF WHICH YOU HAVE *EVER* MENTIONED TO ME *DESPITE* THE FACT THAT WE VOWED TO TAKE *NO* CASE WITHOUT *DISCUSSION.*

WHO ARE THESE PEOPLE? WHAT'S ON THIS *VIDEOTAPE?*

I DIDN'T WANT TO SAY UNTIL IT WAS A SURE THING. YOU'RE FORCING MY HAND.

HELL, YES, I AM.

"OKAY. START AGAIN. FORTKNIGHT'S A PREDATOR CORPORATION POSING AS A NO-STRINGS *ENDOWMENT* FUND.

"THEY STAKE PROMISING YOUNG *INVENTORS*...THEN *BURY* THEM WITH BOGUS *OWNERSHIP* CLAIMS, PATENT INFRINGEMENT ALLEGATIONS, AND *WORSE* WHENEVER THEIR 'BENEFICIARIES' STRIKE *GOLD.*

...

FINE.

THE VIDEO S SOME AMATEUR MCORDER FOOTAGE I N AT AUCTION A WHILE . BEEN HOLDING ONTO IT IN CASE YOU EVER...WELL...

"*ELLIOT PASKO'S* ONE OF THEIR *VICTIMS.* GOOD KID, FLAT BROKE. HE CAME TO US HAT IN HAND, AND WHEN I SAW HIS *WORK,* WE MADE A DEAL:

"ALL THE PRO BONO HE *REQUIRED* IN EXCHANGE FOR TEN PERCENT OF FUTURE PROFITS.

"IT'S STILL IN VERY EARLY *PROTOTYPE,* MATT, BUT SOMEDAY HIS INVENTION'S GOING TO CHANGE THE *WORLD.*"

"IF IT'S WORTH KILLING PASKO'S *LAWYER* OVER, THEN I IMAGINE. YOU SHOULD HAVE TOLD ME, FOGGY. WHY DID YOU GO TO STUPID LENGTHS TO KEEP IT A SECRET?"

"I THOUGHT IT WAS WORTH IT. BECAUSE LET ME ASK YOU SOMETHING NOW. YOU'VE BEEN BLIND SINCE YOU WERE A KID.

"IF YOU COULD HAVE YOUR SIGHT BACK, MATT...FOR JUST, LIKE, HALF AN HOUR...

"...AND YOU COULD SEE *ONE THING* YOU *MISSED,* PAST OR PRESENT...WHAT WOULD IT BE?"

"I DON'T KNOW."

"I BET I DO."

What eventually happened to Pasko and his invention... that's a whole different story.

And I'd rather not spend the rest of the night wallowing in memory.

Someone picked at my father's grave, and they'll be sorry.

Someone's trying to turn Foggy *against* me, and that'll go even *worse* for them.

Because I'm not letting *anyone* threaten what I finally *have* after all these years and years of being *beaten down*.

For the first time in a long while, I *like* my life. I like who I *am*.

I'm a *winner*.

Just like my dad.

EIGHTEEN

I...I HEAR YOU PEOPLE ARE *CONSULTANTS.*

YOU'LL TEACH PEOPLE TO *DEFEND* THEMSELVES IN COURT WHEN THEY CANNOT GET A *LAWYER.*

PLEASE HELP ME.

YOU'VE CHOSEN A *BAD* TIME TO STOP BY, MR. SANTIAGO.

FIRST OFF, THIS IS AFTER-HOURS.

MORE IMPORTANTLY, WE DON'T DO THAT SORT OF THING ANYMORE NOW THAT MR. MURDOCK IS NO LONGER WITH THE *FIRM.*

YOU ARE NOT MURDOCK--?

I AM FRANKLIN NELSON. IF YOU ARE ABOUT TO INQUIRE AS TO MR. MURDOCK'S WHEREABOUTS, TRUST ME, YOU WOULD NEED AN ELECTRON MICROSCOPE TO MEASURE MY *INTEREST.*

I NEED HELP. IT'S NOT FOR ME. IT'S FOR MY SISTER. SHE IS IN TROUBLE OVER THE *HIERRA* KILLING. THE *WORST* KIND OF TROUBLE.

YOUR SISTER IS *ADELE SANTIAGO?*

SI. YOU KNOW OF--?

I FOLLOW THE NEWS.

I'LL GIVE YOU FIVE MINUTES.

I ASSUME YOU'RE HERE BECAUSE YOUR SISTER'S STICKING TO HER STORY, WHICH IS SO UNBELIEVABLE THAT IT *MUST* HAVE GOTTEN GARBLED BY THE PRESS.

SO WHY DON'T YOU TELL IT TO ME EXACTLY AS, I'M SURE, SHE TOLD IT TO *YOU*?

VERY WELL. FOR THE LAST TWO YEARS, ADELE WAS A NURSE AND PHYSICAL THERAPIST TO MR. *VICTOR HIERRA.*

DRUG KINGPIN.

NELSON ~~MURDOCK~~ ATTORNEYS AT LAW

Victor Hierra

"I'M SORRY, 'BUSINESSMAN.' TELL ME STRAIGHT, MR. SANTIAGO, WAS ADELE INVOLVED IN *ANY* UNSAVORY--?"

"*NO.* SHE ATTENDED STRICTLY TO MR. HIERRA'S CHRONIC *MEDICAL NEEDS,* WHICH WERE *MANY.* DIABETES, PALSY, BRITTLE BONES...

"...ADELE WAS ON CALL THAT NIGHT, AS SHE OFTEN WAS. HIERRA WAS A VERY CAUTIOUS MAN.

"HE VALUED *SECURITY.* ADELE SAID HIS INNER OFFICE WAS A *FORTRESS.*"

FLUMP

SLAM

KCHAK

SSSHKK

LOCKED FROM THE *INSIDE*. JUST THE *TWO* OF THEM, ADELE AND HIERRA. FOR HOW LONG?

ABOUT AN HOUR.

DURING WHICH?

ADELE SIMPLY TENDED TO HER *DUTIES*...

"...SORTING PILLS, CHARTING DOSAGES, RECORDING CALORIE COUNTS AND OTHER SUCH THINGS.

"IT WAS HER JOB TO KEEP HIERRA IN THE PINK OF HEALTH, AND SHE TOOK HER RESPONSIBILITIES *SERIOUSLY*.

"SHE SAW NOTHING. THIS I KNOW, BECAUSE I WAS ON THE PHONE WITH HER AT THE TIME IT *HAPPENED*. SHE SIMPLY HEARD THE OLD MAN *FALL*.

"FEARING A STROKE OR A SEIZURE, SHE RAN TO HIS SIDE, BUT SHE WAS TOO *LATE*.

"HIERRA WAS LYING *DEAD* ON A *DRY* AND *SPOTLESS* CARPET--

"--HIS BODY DRAINED *HEAD TO TOE* OF EVERY OUNCE OF BLOOD."

HOW? *HOW* COULD THAT *POSSIBLY* HAVE--

THAT IS WHAT HIERRA'S *BODYGUARDS* DEMANDED TO KNOW.

"THEY POUNCED ON MY SISTER, THREATENED HER. THE DOORS AND WINDOWS WERE STILL LOCKED. THAT MEANT SHE MUST BE *INVOLVED*, THEY INSISTED.

"THEY ACCUSED HER OF BEING *COMPLICIT* IN THIS IMPOSSIBLE CRIME, OF BEING PAID TO *BETRAY* HIERRA. THEY *BEAT* HER. WHEN SHE WOULD NOT 'CONFESS,' THEY HAD HER *ARRESTED.*"

SHE IS BEING HELD WITHOUT BAIL, CHARGED AS AN *ACCESSORY* TO MURDER DESPITE MY PROTESTS.

I WAS *"THERE,"* SO TO SPEAK, THOUGH THE D.A. SAYS THAT PROVES NOTHING. BUT I HEARD ADELE'S SURPRISE AND HORROR WITH MY OWN EARS, MR. NELSON.

AS GOD IS MY WITNESS, SHE IS INNOCENT.

I MUST DEFEND HER.

BECAUSE YOU CAN'T AFFORD THE KIND OF LAWYER WHO'LL STAND UP TO A HIERRA SYNDICATE OUT FOR VENGEANCE?

YEAH. THOUGHT NOT.

SHE'S ENTITLED BY LAW TO A PUBLIC DEFENDER. WAS SOMEONE APPOINTED?

A MAN NAMED ROBERT RANNEY.

OH, HELL. RANNEY'S IN THE SYNDICATE'S POCKET, BOUGHT AND PAID FOR.

I SUSPECTED. HE BARELY MAKES AN EFFORT. YOU MUST TEACH ME WHAT I NEED TO KNOW.

‹SIGH›

MR. SANTIAGO, THIS ISN'T A DISPUTE OVER A NEIGHBOR'S FENCE. THIS IS WAY ABOVE YOUR PAY GRADE. I CAN'T TEACH YOU.

... I SEE.

I'M SORRY I BOTHERED YOU.

APOLOGIZE TO MY GIRLFRIEND. SHE'S THE ONE WHO'S GONNA HIT THE ROOF WHEN SHE FINDS OUT I'M POSTPONING OUR VACATION SO I CAN TAKE YOUR CASE.

I-I-I HAVE NO MONEY--

YEAH, WELL, "I-I-I" HAVE NO CHOICE.

SEE, MY EX-PARTNER WAS A HUMAN LIE DETECTOR, AND WHILE IT KILLS ME TO ADMIT THIS RIGHT NOW--OH, YOU HAVE NO IDEA--

--OVER THE YEARS, I LEARNED A GREAT DEAL FROM MATT MURDOCK ABOUT HOW TO SPOT A LIAR. AND YOU'RE NOT ONE.

YOU'RE TELLING THE TRUTH, AND I CAN'T LET YOUR SISTER BE FALSELY CONVICTED.

STUPID MATT.

WHEREVER YOU ARE...

"...I HOPE YOU'RE *MISERABLE.*"

...AND THAT'S APPARENTLY THE PRICE I PAY FOR BEING OFF THE *GRID* A FEW DAYS, KIRSTEN.

FOGGY'S LIVID.

HE WAS PROBABLY *WORRIED* ABOUT YOU. YOUR LIFE WAS *THREATENED.*

DAREDEVIL CLEARED THAT UP FOR ME.

I'M SURE HE *DID.* "TELL HIM I SAID *THANKS,*" SHE SAID, SARCASTICALLY.

"I *WILL,*" HE COUNTERED, NOT RISING TO THE *BAIT.*

SERIOUSLY... THANKS FOR SEEING ME. AND SEEING ME *HOME.*

I'M JUST *FULL* OF GOOD DEEDS THEY'RE NOT *EXHAUSTED...*

YOU...SHOULD GO *HOME.* IT'S *LATE.*

UMM... OKAY...?

I'M *SORRY.*

I'M JUST NOT...FEELING WELL.

G'NIGHT.

WHAT THE *HELL...?*

MATT?

MATT, IS THAT YOU...?

She can't...

...*be* here...

...this isn't *happening*...

I recognize the woman in my bed.

By her heartbeat. By her voice. By the way the air tastes when she's around me.

By all the other little things that made me love her enough to *marry* her.

MATT, YOU'RE *SCARING* ME. WHAT'S *WRONG*...?

What's wrong is that you're supposed to be upstate in a *mental institution*, Milla.

What's *wrong* is that one of my enemies drove you *insane* just to *hurt* me, and your parents never *forgave* me.

What's *wrong* is that once you were committed, once they found there was no cure for your madness...

...they sued for *custody*, had our marriage *annulled* and you permanently *committed*, and slapped me with a *restraining order* and now you're in my bedroom.

MATT, SAY *SOMETHING*--!

STOP. JUST...

...STOP.

MILLA, HOW DID YOU GET IN THIS APARTMENT?

HOW...?

I *LIVE* HERE, SWEETHEART.

MATT, YOU'RE FRIGHTENING ME. COME HERE. PUT YOUR ARMS AROUND ME. PLEASE.

WHY WON'T YOU?

Because I'm afraid I'll never let go.

MILLA... HONEY...YOU *CAN'T BE HERE.* THEY'LL THINK I *TOOK* YOU.

I COULD BE DISBARRED. I COULD GO TO *JAIL.*

"TOOK ME"? FROM WHERE? YOU'RE MAKING NO SENSE. THIS IS OUR HOME, SWEETHEART!

She remembers nothing, but she's getting agitated, which makes her violent. That leaves me no choice but to...

YOU'RE RIGHT, MILLA. NEVER MIND. I'VE JUST... I'VE GOT A HEADACHE.

LET ME MAKE US SOME TEA.

I'LL BE RIGHT THERE...

...AND EVERYTHING WILL BE JUST FINE.

"IT'S ME."

"I KNOW YOU SAID NOT TO CALL FOR A WHILE."

"BUT I'M IN VERY DEEP TROUBLE."

I KNOW YOU'RE THERE, FOGGY. I CAN HEAR YOU SWEATING.

OKAY, I'M GUESSING ABOUT THE SWEAT, BUT YOU HAVE TO ADMIT, THE ODDS ARE PRETTY G--

DON'T DO THAT. DON'T TRY TO JOKE THE AWKWARDNESS AWAY. LET ME SAVOR IT.

FORGET YOU. YOU WANT HELP, CALL THE AVENGERS--

IT'S ABOUT MILLA.

...

PARDON?

I CAME HOME TO FIND HER IN MY APARTMENT, CONFUSED AS HELL AND ACTING LIKE NOTHING...BAD EVER HAPPENED.

I DON'T KNOW HOW SHE FOUND HER WAY HERE OR WHAT TO DO WITH HER.

I GAVE HER ENOUGH SEDATIVE TO KNOCK HER OUT FOR THE NEXT FEW HOURS SO SHE'LL BE SAFE, BUT DO I JUST MOVE HER? TO WHERE?

FOGGY, YOU'VE GOT TO DROP EVERYTHING AND GO TO THE ASYLUM RIGHT NOW--FIND OUT HOW SHE GOT OUT.

YOU HAVE SOME NERVE.

NO, SCRATCH THAT. YOU HAVE *ALL* THE NERVE *BETWEEN* US BECAUSE YOU'VE WORN MY LAST ONE TO *NOTHING.*

THEN DON'T DO THIS FOR ME. DO IT FOR MILLA.

FOGGY, I'M BEGGING YOU. I CAN'T TRUST ANYONE ELSE WITH THIS REQUEST. YOU *ALONE* KNOW HOW SENSITIVE A MATTER THIS IS.

FOGGY, PLEASE. THERE'S NO ONE ELSE I CAN TURN TO.

FOR MILLA. IN RETURN, YOU DO TWO THINGS FOR *ME.*

NAME THEM.

FIRST, CHECK YOUR E-MAIL. I'M SENDING INFORMATION ON A RECENT *MOB HIT.* DAREDEVIL OUGHT TO NOSE AROUND SO AN INNOCENT NURSE DOESN'T GET *LIFE...*OR GET *WHACKED.*

I'LL CALL YOU IN A BIT, WE'LL COMPARE NOTES, AFTER WHICH YOU DO THE *SECOND* THING:

"LOSE MY NUMBER."

This is good. I need to clear my head and make a *plan.*

I'm *drastically* off my game.

Someone robbed my father's grave and left his remains in my *office...*

...leaving Foggy-- who's been *questioning* my sanity--convinced that *I'd* done it and *lied* about it.

But it was an impossible theft. Dad's coffin was stolen and trashed by the *Mole Man.**

*BACK IN DD #9-#10.

Revenge from *him?* I checked, but no. The Avengers said he'd been busy warring on Ulik the Troll since last we fought.

I went...*asking around* on a more *local* level, but no one had any intel to give. Case was a dead end. *No one* could have retrieved Dad's remains *but* me. And it *wasn't* me.

Was it?

No. Focus. Find *Hierra's* murderer. Why was he killed?

Let's make sure it wasn't simply an issue of *job performance.*

LOOK AT ALL THE NEIGHBORHOODS YOU CAN SEE FROM UP HERE, BENNY.

NEED IT... GOT IT... NEED IT...GOT IT...GOT IT...

GOT IT.

Jardiem Salazar has made a name for himself by importing narcotics from south of the border and setting up shop in New York's rougher areas.

He is-- *was*--Hierra's overlord.

He has a reputation for not suffering perceived incompetence among his underlings.

And he's not above a random "*firing*" once or twice a year just to remind them who's *boss*.

Who works for a man like that on *purpose?*

EVENING, MR. SALAZAR. THIS WEEK'S P-AND-L'S ARE IN. YOU SAID YOU WANTED THEM RIGHT AWAY...?

EVERYONE'S AT QUOTA BUT *WOMACK.* I WARNED THAT LAZY...

REMOVE HIM FROM THE PAYROLL. HIM *AND* HIS WIFE.

LET THAT BE A *LESSON* FOR THE *OTHERS.*

LIKE *HIERRA* WAS?

JUST GIVE ME AN *ANSWER,* SAL. DON'T MAKE ME *PULL* IT OUT OF YOU.

DAREDEVIL!

BLAM
BLAM
BLAM-
BLAM

KAK

PAF

DON'T WASTE MY TIME.

ZWIIIP

AND DON'T TRY TO BILL ME FOR THE FURNITURE.

WE HEARD SHOTS--!

A HUNDRED THOUSAND TO THE MAN WHO BLOWS HIS BRAINS OUT! GO!

This is why it's dumb to *surround* a man who can "see" 360 degrees.

No matter which way I move, I've got something to *hit*.

WHUMP

That
scream--

--he's falling
down the
shaft--?

--where was
the *elevator
car*--?

Come on,
come on--

--catch
him with the
*grapple-
line*--

CHNNK

How did he--?

Trap door--or *something*--how did he *fall* from a *closed* elevator--?

Foggy's pulsebuzz.

I HAVE NEWS. YOU FIRST, THOUGH.

FOGGY? YOU THERE?

tap
tap

TELL ME YOU WERE JUST *PRANKING* ME, MATT.

WHAT ARE YOU TALKING ABOUT?

PLEASE TELL ME YOU WERE JOKING.

I WASN'T. ARE YOU AT THE HOSPITAL?

YEAH. AND YOU'RE GONNA BE, TOO, MATT! I'M GOING TO *HAVE* YOU *COMMITTED* FOR YOUR *OWN GOOD!*

FOGGY, I'M NOT *CRAZY*--

YES, YOU *ARE!* I DON'T CARE *WHAT* YOU THINK YOU *HALLUCINATED* TONIGHT, MATT, BUT IT *WASN'T YOUR EX-WIFE*--

NINETEEN

The billy club. It was *here*. I *know* it was holstered.

...

Wasn't it?

YOU'VE LOST YOUR MIND, MATT.

Of course it was. I'm more protective of that thing than Captain America is of his *shield*.

I didn't lose it!

I'M NOT CRAZY!

PAF

KE-WNNK

Hope that's on my tombstone.

CRASH

...where...?

...my apartment...?

How in the world--?

MILLA.

I locked her in the *bedroom* not an hour ago--!

MILLA!

Not only is she *gone*, but it's as if she were never *here*.

The bed's the way I make it--Milla never could learn the hospital corner--and the sheets smell of detergent, not of *her*.

Maybe Foggy's onto something. I think I'm fine, but history would argue that I'm not always the best judge of my own mental state.

I need to see a doctor.

I should take a cab.

AVENGERS TOWER.

WHAT DO YOU MEAN THERE'S SOMETHING WRONG WITH MY BRAIN?

I DIDN'T SAY "WRONG."

Hank Pym, a.k.a. Giant-Man, a.k.a. Ant-Man, a.k.a. what day is it, recently operated on my gray matter...from the inside.

He is not comforting.

I SAID I GOT SOME ODD READINGS WHEN I WAS OPERATING IN THERE.

"EVEN AT MICROSCOPIC SIZE, MY INSTRUMENTS WERE DETECTING A UNIQUE RADIATION SIGNATURE.

"I ASSUMED IT WAS JUST PART AND PARCEL OF YOUR RADAR SENSE, BUT MAYBE NOT."

SOMETHING COULD BE GOING ON IN THERE TO CAUSE HALLUCINATIONS.

OKAY. NO. WAIT. THAT WOULDN'T ACCOUNT FOR MY DAD'S SKULL.

EXCUSE ME?

FOGGY DISCOVERED MY DEAD FATHER'S REMAINS IN MY DESK DRAWER AFTER I TOLD HIM THEY WERE GONE FOREVER.

HE'S CONVINCED I WAS LYING TO HIM AND/OR TO MYSELF, AND...

...AND MAYBE HE'S RIGHT. I DON'T KNOW.

I JUST DON'T KNOW.

IF IT'S A BIOCHEMICAL ISSUE, IT CAN BE FIXED. FIRST STEP IS TO REST.

CAN'T. NOT WHILE THERE'S AN INNOCENT WOMAN ON TRIAL FOR HER LIFE.

PRIVATE NURSE. ACCORDING TO FOGGY, SHE'S BEEN CHARGED AS AN ACCESSORY TO THE MURDER OF A *DRUGLORD*.

HOW'D HE DIE?

BELIEVE IT OR NOT, *SPONTANEOUS EXSANGUINATION*. ACCORDING TO THE NURSE, OUR SOLE *WITNESS*, ALL THE BLOOD IN THE VICTIM'S BODY SUDDENLY...

...

...DISAPPEARED...

...SON OF A...!

THAT'S GOT TO BE *IT*. CAN YOU RUN AN *AT-LARGE* FOR ME? I CAN'T WORK THOSE THINGS.

SURE. WHAT ARE WE LOOKING FOR?

SOMEONE WITH AN *AXE* TO GRIND WHO'S SMARTER THAN I *TOOK* HIM FOR.

AND IF I'M *RIGHT*...

"...I KNOW HIS *NEXT* TARGET."

FIRST ROUND'S ON ME, OKAY?

NOPE. I OWE YOU. PLUS, THIS INN'T MY FIRST ROUND.

FOGGY, HOW LONG HAVE YOU *BEEN* HERE?

TOO LONG.

AND, STILL, YOU EXPECT A TIP.

FORGET HIM. KIRSTEN, THANK YOU FOR MEETING ME SO'S I CAN *APOLOGIZE.*

FOR...?

FOR *MATTHEW MICHAEL MURDOCK.* AND LETTING YOU GET *INVOLVED* WITH HIM.

YOU DIDN'T "*LET*" ME GET--

I DIDN'T THROW MYSELF ON TH' GRENADE, NNNNEITHER. I'M *SO SORRY,* KIRSTEN...

...C'N YOU KEEP A *SECRET* 'BOUT MATT?

IT...*DEPENDS.* I THINK WE SHOULD CHANGE THE *SUBJ--*

THAT...*OTHER GUY* YOU THINK MATT IS SOMETIMES?

YOU'RE *RIGHT.*

HE'S CLIMBIN' ROOFS EVEN NOW. BUT YOU GOTTA KNOW THE *REST,* S'YOU DON' THINK IT'S YOU...

...AND I GOTTA TELL *SOMEBODY* 'CAUSE IT'S *KILLIN'* ME. 'KAY?

FOGGY, DON'T--

MATT'S GONE *CRAZY!* NO JOKE! HE *SNAPPED* LIKE I WAS *SCARED* HE WOULD, *KNEW* HE WOULD...AND HE DESP'RATELY NEEDS *PSYCHIATRIC* HELP.

...

WHAT?

FOGGY, THINK ABOUT WHAT YOU JUST *SAID!*

I AM AN *ASSISTANT DISTRICT ATTORNEY!* I AM AN OFFICER OF THE *COURT* WITH A SWORN RESPONSIBILITY TOWARDS *PUBLIC SAFETY!*

AND YOU JUST TOLD ME THAT *DAREDEVIL* HAS GONE *INSANE* AND THAT HE IS *AT LARGE* IN THIS CITY AND QUITE POSSIBLY *DANGEROUS!*

NO... WAIT...OH, *GOD,* THAT'S NOT WHAT I--

FOGGY, UNLESS YOU TELL ME *RIGHT NOW* THAT YOU ARE *DRUNK* AND *ANGRY* AND YOU ARE TALKING *THROUGH YOUR HAT...*

...I HAVE *NO CHOICE* BUT TO HAVE MY OFFICE BEGIN A *CITYWIDE MANHUNT* FOR MATT'S *OWN GOOD!*

WELL?

HE *NEEDS* HELP.

DON'T HURT MY FRIEND.

DAREDEVIL--?

IT'S A TRAP!

I'LL SAY. BUT NOT *MINE*.

WE HAVE A COMMON ENEMY. HE'S TORMENTING ME, AND HE'S SETTING HIMSELF UP TO REPLACE ALL OF *YOU*.

GATHERING UNDER *ONE* ROOF MAKES HIS JOB *SIMPLER*.

PLEASE, VIGILANTE. WE ARE NOT *SIMPLE MEN*. WE ARE AWARE OF THE RISKS, BUT WE ARE ADEQUATELY PROTECTED.

IF THAT'S WHAT YOU REALLY BELIEVE...

...THEN YOU HAVE NO IDEA WHAT YOU'RE *UP* AGAINST.

NOTHING WE CANNOT HANDLE--

QUIET!

There it is:

Like his signature.

A half-decibel shift in the acoustics.

He's here.

GET DOWN! GET

DOWN!

?

His name is *The Spot--*

NIEEEE

--and he is
done for.

Where's the *don?* I was right *behind* him--!

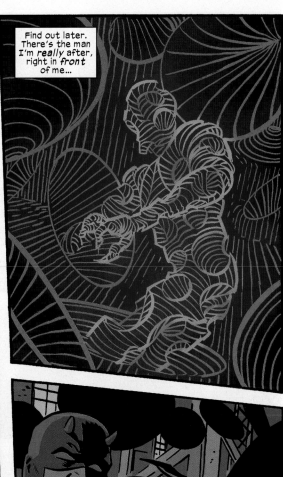

Find out later. There's the man I'm *really* after, right in *front* of me...

...and he's brought some *helping hands--!*

?

Sound of my pulse...

...of chains clinking...

...why are they so *faint?*

Why--

SPOT! YOU'RE A DEAD MAN--!

I'M A *NEW* MAN.

TWENTY

I knew him as the *Spot*.

CALL ME COYOTE.

Whether after the *predator* or the *Trickster God*, it doesn't *matter*. Either *fits*.

He's been using his *teleportation powers* to create *chaos* among the New York underworld--

--and to torment me into questioning my own sanity...

...by moving *people* and *things* around like *props* in a macabre *one-act*.

After single-handedly slaughtering a warehouse full of *crime bosses* like ducks in a *shooting gallery*, he lured me through one of his *portals*--

--locked some sort of *electronic collar* around my neck--

--and used it to separate my *head* from my *body*.

And that's when I knew I'd *won*.

Another change: he *speaks* now. Good.

I absolutely have to keep him *talking*.

A hostile line of questioning should do it...

SO...*YOU'VE* COME UP IN THE WORLD. I GUESS I OWE SPIDER-MAN *TWENTY BUCKS.*

DECIDED TO TAKE OVER THE TRI-STATE *DRUG TRADE*, I GATHER?

NOT MY STYLE.

HOW SO? IT'S NOT A *ROAD RUNNER CARTOON?*

What makes it easy to stay relatively calm is that I can still feel my body...still control it.

I'm just glad I can't *see* it.

That would freak me out.

TOO MUCH *FUSS.* I *HAVE* BEGUN *ONE* SOLO ENTERPRISE, BUT WE'LL GET TO THAT. BY AND LARGE, I'M STILL A *CONTRACTOR* AT HEART. WORK FOR HIRE, AND ALL THAT.

BUT SINCE THERE'S NOTHING CLIENTS CAN *PAY* ME THAT I CAN'T SIMPLY *TAKE*...

...I CHOOSE TO HAVE *FUN* WITH MY *WORK.*

UNDER *THAT* PHILOSOPHY, MY FIRST NEW CLIENT WAS AN ASPIRING KURDISH *WARLORD.*

"HE WAS HAVING DIFFICULTY SMUGGLING *ASSAULT* WEAPONS IN FROM A NEIGHBORING COUNTRY..."

"...SO I REOPENED HIS *SUPPLY LINE.*"

<THERE THEY *ARE!*>*

*TRANSLATED FROM KURDISH.

<TRACE THE TUNNEL *BACK* TO ITS *SOURCE!* GO! GO!>

"I SUPPOSE I COULD HAVE HOOKED HIM UP WITH A NEW, MORE *DIRECT* ROUTE..."

<NOWHERE TO GO BUT TOWARDS THE *BORDER,* IS THERE?>

<RACE YOU.>

"ONE OF THE WORLD'S LARGEST *ARCOTICS SYNDICATES*, THEY'D BEEN LOOKING TO TAKE A BITE OUT OF THE *BIG APPLE.*

"THEY'D BEEN USING *DRUG MULES* TO SMUGGLE MERCHANDISE THROUGH *LA GUARDIA...*

"...BUT, REALISTICALLY, HOW MANY 'PREGNANT' WOMEN CAN YOU MOVE THROUGH CUSTOMS IN ONE DAY WITHOUT AROUSING SUSPICION?

"HOW MANY PER FLIGHT?

"NO. THEIR PROCESS WAS TRIED AND TRUE, BUT INEFFICIENT.

"I SHOWED THEM ONE WAY TO WIDEN THE *PIPELINE.*

SO NOW THEY'RE FUNNELING ENOUGH PRODUCT TO FEEL CONFIDENT IN ELIMINATING LOCAL *RIVALS*.

THEY HIRED YOU TO OFF HIERRA, SALAZAR... *TORTINO* AND HIS BOYS...

WHY GO ALL *LOCKED-ROOM MYSTERY* WITH THE KILLINGS? WHY THE *THEATRICS*? WHY NOT JUST 'PORT THEM TO THE BOTTOM OF THE *ATLANTIC*?

ONLY *YOU* WOULD HAVE TO *ASK*.

BECAUSE I'M TRYING TO INSTILL *FEAR*.

EH. YOU DIDN'T THINK THAT WOULD WORK ON ME, TOO? PLAYING GAMES WITH ME, RATTLING MY SANITY. IF YOU WANT *VENGEANCE* FOR MY *HUMILIATING* YOU, WHY NOT *KILL* ME?

BECAUSE THAT WASN'T THE *ASSIGNMENT*.

Assignment?

Press him. You've got him positioned. Don't let the witness leave the *stand*...

YOU SAID SOMETHING ABOUT A *SOLO* OPERATION. THAT'S UNCHARACTERISTICALLY AMBITIOUS.

A MAN HAS TO HAVE A *HOBBY*.

DO YOU KNOW WHAT THE FASTEST-GROWING CRIMINAL INDUSTRY IN THE *WORLD* IS?

I do. And now he's made me *angry*.

HUMAN TRAFFICKING.

SECOND ONLY TO THE **DRUG TRADE** IN PROFITABILITY...

...ESPECIALLY IF *I'M* THE ONLY ONE WHO **PROFITS.**

NOW, FINDING ENOUGH **VICTIMS**...

"...KIDNAPPING ENOUGH WOULD-BE SLAVES TO SUPPLY ALL THE WORLD'S DIAMOND-MINERS AND SHARECROPPERS AND DRAFTEES AND..."

"...WELL... WHAT-HAVE-YOU..."

"...PROCUREMENT'S NOT AN ISSUE GIVEN MY ABILITIES."

That noise... what's that *noise*...?

BUT FIGURING OUT A WAY TO KEEP ALL THAT HUMAN CHATTEL **DOCILE** ENOUGH FOR ME TO **CONTROL**...

...UNABLE TO **RESIST** OR **REBEL** WHILE BEING SHOPPED **AROUND**...

"...THAT TOOK A WHILE TO CRACK."

It's coming from behind the *door*.

And it's *deafening*.

By *anyone's* standards.

Oh, God.

TWELVE NOON.

FEEDING TIME.

Even I can't find the words to express my rage and disgust, and I am *very* good at that.

Every victim in the room is screaming as if caught in the fires of *hell itself.*

And if they're looking to me for *any* sort of relie at *all*, I wish I could *tell* them..

...that it's *coming.*

THE OFFICE OF DISTRICT ATTORNEY CYRUS BARGER.

≩SIGH≩

COME IN, KIRSTEN.

YOU'RE IN THE MIDDLE OF A MEETING. IT CAN WAIT--

NO, NO. YOU'VE DECLARED THIS AN *URGENT MATTER*, SO FILL ME *IN*.

POLICE CHIEF DANFORTH, SENATOR MAYWRIGHT...YOU'VE MET ASSISTANT D.A. MCDUFFIE?

I'VE HEARD THE NAME.

ON TMZ.

I'D--RATHER TALK ONE-ON-ONE--

THEN SEE ME *THURSDAY*. OTHERWISE, *SPEAK*.

ALL RIGHT. WE'LL NEED THE CHIEF'S HELP, ANYWAY.

SIR, IT'S ABOUT *DAREDEVIL*. I'VE BEEN RELIABLY INFORMED THAT HE'S BECOME SOMEWHAT... MENTALLY *UNBALANCED*. THAT HIS ERRATIC BEHAVIOR COULD POTENTIALLY BE A DANGER TO PUBLIC SAFETY.

I WOULD SUGGEST YOU ASK THE POLICE TO ISSUE AN A.P.B. AND BRING HIM IN FOR *QUESTIONING*.

A SPLENDID IDEA, I'M SURE, DEAR...

TIK TAK

...BUT WE HAVE MORE IMPORTANT THINGS TO DO THAN INTERFERE IN A *LOVERS'* QUARREL.

NYScene
by Miriam Birchwood

LAWYERS IN LOVE?
Daredevil Alter-Ego Matt Murdock Cozies Up With Assistant D.A.

I *WARNED* YOU ABOUT HOW YOUR CHOICE OF *BOYFRIENDS* MIGHT COME *ACROSS*, DID I *NOT*?

WHAT? HE'S NOT MY--

THAT'S *ABSURD!* WE HAVE A *SERIOUS* PROBLEM!

I'M SURE YOU DO. YOU KNOW WHO GIVES GOOD RELATIONSHIP ADVICE? *DAN SAVAGE.* WRITE TO HIM. I HAVE WORK TO DO.

DID YOU SEE HER *FACE?* BOY, SHE WAS *PISSED!*

HEY, BARGER, MY KID'S MAKING ME NUTS. CAN YOU BRING *HIM* IN?

WONDER WHO SHE'S GONNA CRY TO *NOW...?*

Coyote's trap is gruesomely clever, no question.

But it has *one flaw*. Unlike *him*...

...it's powered *artificially*.

I detected an anomaly--a unique *stutter* in the air the moment I first came *to*.

A broadcast energy with a frequency in sync with a faint *thrumming* beneath my boots.

Something in this compound--some *machine*--is keeping Coyote's victims helpless by severing them from their *senses*.

SNAK

After all, what are their bodies going to do without *sight*?

CHAK

Just grope *around*?

HMM.
THAT'S
ODD.

Damn it.

YOU GOT
AWFULLY
QUIET ALL OF
A SUDDEN.

SOMETHING
ON YOUR
MIND?

LET'S
SEE WHERE
YOU'VE *RUN*
TO, SHALL
WE?

Nothing obvious to the touch. Time to start *breaking* everything I can *grab* and pray for the *best*.

...stopped dividing my attention. He's *on* to me.

AAAAH. WELL PLAYED.

CHNK

NO! GET AWAY FROM THERE--!

NO!

CLIK

?

In my time, I've fought off Kingpin, Bullseye, and the *Hulk*.

I am *not* dying like *this*.

I thought I could trap *Coyote* and *then* tend to his confused, freed prisoners--but they found him *first. And* me.

And their *adrenaline stench* and their panicked *keening* tells me that, given their ordeal, they're not to be *reasoned* with immediately.

After all Coyote has put me through, I'm tempted to save my *own* skin and leave him to the *mob*--

--but I need him to explain what his connection is to *The Spot*.

I need to find out who set him *against* me.

And most of all...

...I need him to clear the innocent woman he framed for *murder*.

Paf

One of two things can happen here, and I'll take *either*.

I can pull myself *free* by hooking on to the cables of the *teleport machine--*

SNAP SNAP

--or they'll tear *loose--*

--and create some I'd-presume-spectacular fireworks--

BZZZZZZZZ

--to scare the mob away.

I haven't the first clue where we *are* in the world, but I trust they'll find their way to an *exit*...

...unless...

Tag that. I have a *new* problem.

The machine must have been using the *Spot* as a "battery," because its *broadcast wavelength* is fading.

It's slowly powering *down*. The collar trapping *Coyote* is already pulsing erratically.

Once it *deactivates* there'll be no way to keep him from *disappearing*, and I'll have *lost*.

Think, Matt. Take a breath and *think*.

At least you're not in *immediate* peril.

...

What was that?

Echoes in the room suddenly *changed.* The *Spot...*

...where'd he *go?*

He could be literally *anywhere.*

THEN "THEY" SENT YOU AFTER *ME?* IS *THAT* IT?

I don't hear an *answer.*

But what I *do* hear...

GYAH!

WELL?

YES! THEY HAD ME *WATCHING* YOU!

I KNEW WHAT TO 'PORT AROUND THAT WOULD *FREAK* WITH YOU! YOUR OLD MAN'S *BONES,* YOUR EX-WIFEA*AAHHH!*

AND "THEY" HAD YOU TARGETING THE *NEW YORK DRUGLORDS* WITH YOUR *TELEPORTALS*, DIDN'T THEY? HIERRA? *SALAZAR?*

YOU OPENED UP THE *FLOOR* OF *SALAZAR'S ELEVATOR!* YOU DRAINED HIERRA'S *BLOOD* FROM *AFAR* AND LEFT HIS *NURSE* TO TAKE THE *FALL!*

DO YOU *ADMIT* THOSE THINGS?

Y--

THWAM

⇒HNNGH⇐

--YES! YES! YOU ALREADY *KNOW ALL* THAT!

TRUE.

AND NOW *THEY* DO, *TOO.*

The prisoners are still *here.* There *is* no exit to the hideout.

Makes sense, I suppose. Why would a man who can *teleport* build an *exterior door?*

Running out of time *fast.*

And I'm down to *one idea,* so it's *all-in.*

HRAK

KRUT

The machine powers the *collars.*

The *collars* create agonizing *feedback* on teleporters.

And when *Coyote's* prisoners were *sprung...*

...they left behind *dozens* of collars!

For a long second, nothing much *happens.*

God keeps me in *suspense.*

But then it gets *ugly.*

Beautifully ugly.

GNAAAAGH!

And then--

AAAACHHAAAAA!

YOU'RE CAUGHT IN A *BACKLASH!* *HOLD STILL!*

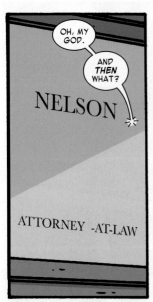

OH, MY GOD.

AND *THEN* WHAT?

NELSON

ATTORNEY -AT-LAW

THEN THE PRISONERS AND I ROUNDED UP ENOUGH HEAVY METAL FOR A MAKESHIFT BATTERING RAM.

"TURNED OUT WE WERE IN ARIZONA, NOT ABSURDLY FAR FROM A HIGHWAY.

"ONCE WE MARCHED TO *CIVILIZATION*, I COULD CONTACT THE *AVENGERS* TO HELP SORT THINGS OUT."

ENOUGH OF COYOTE'S VICTIMS SPOKE *ENGLISH* THAT THE LOCAL COPS WERE ABLE TO GATHER ADMISSIBLE STATEMENTS ABOUT EVERYTHING THEY HEARD AND SAW.

THOSE ENOUGH TO CLEAR YOUR CLIENT?

IT SURE LOOKS SO.

YOU REALLY WERE THE VICTIM IN THIS, MATTY. NOW I GET IT. THIS EXPLAINS EVERYTHING.

EXCEPT WHY YOU'D TURN ON YO *BEST* FRIEND.

MATTY, I APOLOGIZE...

YOU *APOLOGIZE*? IT'S LIKE YOU WERE *READY* TO KNIFE ME! AFTER *ALL THE*--

GOOD GOD, FOGGY, YOU AND I HAVE HAD OUR LIVES TURNED UPSIDE DOWN *HOW MANY* TIMES BY *SYNDICATES* AND *CRIME BOSSES* AND PSYCHOS WITH *AXES* TO GRIND?

WE LIVE IN A WORLD WHERE *GODS OF MYTH* WALK THE STREETS, WHERE *MAGIC SPELLS* CAN SAVE THE DAY--

--AND YOU THREW OUR *FRIENDSHIP* UNDER A BUS BECAUSE SOMEONE FOOLED YOU WITH HIS *SLEIGHT-OF-HAND* ACT?

I THOUGHT YOU'D LIED TO ME. I SHOULD HAVE TRUSTED YOU ON THIS. AND *KIRSTE--*

"*ON THIS*"? HOW ABOUT, "*I SHOULD HAVE TRUSTED YOU, PERIOD*"?

AND WHY DID YOUR *PULSE RATE PUNCH* WHEN YOU MENTIONED *KIRSTEN'S* NAME?

YOU HAVEN'T TALKED TO HER?

SHE WON'T TAKE MY *CALLS*. *WHY IS THAT, FOGGY*?

EXPLAIN YOURSELF BEFORE YOUR DAMN *HEART* EXPLODES!

I HAD TO TALK TO *SOMEBODY*.

I TOLD HER EVERYTHING, MATT.

I TOLD HER YOU'D GONE NUTS. THAT YOU NEEDED HELP.

THAT I COULDN'T GET MATT MURDOCK TO SEEK TREATMENT, BUT *LAW ENFORCEMENT* MIGHT BE ABLE TO BRING *DAREDEVIL* IN FOR OBSERVATION.

YOU TOLD AN ASSISTANT D.A. THAT I WAS A *PUBLIC MENA--*

WHAT IF YOU ARE?

EXCUSE ME?

I'M STILL *SUSPICIOUS.*

WHAT MORE DO YOU *WANT?* COYOTE *PLAYED* YOU! *COYOTE* MOVED MILLA IN AND OUT OF THE *ASYLUM!*

DID HE CURE *YOU* OF A LIFETIME OF SELF-DESTRUCTIVE DEPRESSION?

I'M FINE.

YOU *SAY.* COYOTE'S COYOTE. HERE'S WHAT WORRIES *ME.*

YOU LET YOUR LIFE GET PRETTY *OUT OF HAND* BEFORE YOU PUT ON YOUR *HAPPY* HAT AND DECIDED TO BE GLIB 24/7.

AND THE *ONLY WAY* THAT THE MATT MURDOCK I KNOW--A TORTURED *CATHOLIC* OF *UNIMAGINABLE INTEGRITY--*

--COULD SO UTTERLY ABSOLVE HIMSELF OF *RESPONSIBILITY* FOR--FOR *MILLA*--FOR *BULLSEYE'S* MURDER, FOR SOME *REALLY DEVASTATING CHOICES*--

--IS IF HE'S NOT *HIMSELF* SOMEHOW.

...

ANYTHING YOU WANT TO *ADD* TO THAT?

NO.

REGARDLESS, I SHOULDN'T HAVE COLD-SHOULDERED YOU. IF YOU *WANT* HELP, I'M *HERE*. I...I NEED IT FROM YOU *TOO*. LET'S JUST PUT THIS BEHIND US, OKAY?

GO TO HELL, NELSON.

HEY, C'MON. I'VE KNOWN YOU TOO LONG--

I DON'T *CARE*. IF YOU'RE *THAT CONVINCED* THAT I HAVE BEEN IN *NO WAY* COMPELLED TO *ATONE* FOR MY SINS...

You didn't deserve any of the things that happened to you just because you fell in love with a man who couldn't protect you from his enemies.

If, through some stroke of luck, you are reading this note, don't let your doctors find it. I shouldn't be writing to you at all, I'm told. I should let the wound close.

But you have to know, as I have said before, that I will spend the rest of my days searching for a way to make up for all your pain and suffering.

You have to know that I think of you every day and that I miss you and want you to be well.

MILLA DONOVAN
GARDENS PSYCHIATRIC HOSPITAL
NY POINT, NY 10980

MURDOCK, M

And you have to know that I will never forgive myself for failing you.

OVAN
IATRIC HOSPITAL
10980

TAL

Love, Matt
Love, Matt
Love, Matt
Love, Matt
Love, Matt
Love, Matt

NEW YORK COUNTY COURTHOUSE.

KIRSTEN McDUFFIE?

THAT'S ME. YOU GOT MY MESSAGE, OBVIOUSLY. THANKS FOR MEETING ME.

YOU SAID IT WAS URGENT.

I'M WORRIED ABOUT OUR MUTUAL FRIEND.

--AS AN OFFICER OF THE COURTS, YOU UNDERSTAND.

IT'S *DAREDEVIL*. I HAVE REASON TO BELIEVE THAT HE'S...MENTALLY UNSTABLE.

AND AS A MATTER OF CIVIC DUTY, I'M UNCOMFORTABLE WITH THE THOUGHT OF A *DELUSIONAL VIGILANTE* RUNNING *UNCHECKED* THROUGH THE *CITY STREETS*.

I SEE. WHO ELSE HAVE YOU SPOKEN TO ABOUT THIS?

NO ONE WHO'LL *ACT*. MATT--*DAREDEVIL*--AND I, WE'VE *DATED*, SO MY *SUPERIORS* THINK I'M PURSUING SOME PERSONAL *VENDETTA*.

BUT THAT'S *CRAP*. I WILL ADMIT THAT I DON'T KNOW IF I'M MORE CONCERNED FOR *HIM* OR FOR THOSE HE COMES IN *CONTACT* WITH--

--BUT EITHER WAY, HE *HAS* TO BE *DEALT* WITH. YOU GET THAT, RIGHT?

I UNDERSTAND WHAT YOU'RE ASKING ME TO DO, YES.

I WILL FIND DAREDEVIL...

...AND I WILL CRUSH HIM.

THANK--

WAIT.

WHAT?

NEXT: WEB OF LIES!

DAREDEVIL #16 *LAYOUTS BY CHRIS SAMNEE*

COYOTE CHARACTER AND TECHNOLOGY DESIGNS BY PAOLO RIVERA

DAREDEVIL #18, PAGE 2 *UNUSED PENCILS BY PAOLO RIVERA*

DAREDEVIL #18 *COVER SKETCHES AND INKS BY PAOLO RIVERA*